How to Disar

Keeping Yourself Safe from Egotists

Daryl Seldon

Barry Gray

How to Disarm a Narcissist

Copyright © 2018

ISBN: 9781977036506

Warning and Disclaimer

Publisher Contact

Skinny Bottle Publishing
books@skinnybottle.com

Daryl Seldon

ACKNOWLEDGMENTS

Highest thanks to Leelee my greatest inspiration, my wife Silke, who has saved my life more than once, and for all the teachers and thinkers alive and gone whose thoughts speak through me.

Identifying the narcissist

Many of us have been hurt by those with a narcissistic personality. These persons are manipulative, condescending, absolutist, and transgress on the freedoms of others. In relationships, they are controlling, manipulative, brutally hurtful, sensitive to criticism, and sometimes violent. Many times, they are males. In our attempts to love them, we are repaid with only pain and disappointment. They may even convince you that you are the crazy one when it is they who have a disorder of the mind.

Though men are more likely to be narcissists, sometimes narcissists are females. Female narcissists behave in a similar way but are often more manipulative than violent. They will attack the man's self-esteem, tell him he's not a man, cheat with other, 'better' men, and then take him back to continue to feed on him.

Grandiose versus Vulnerable Narcissists

There can be said to be different types of narcissists. Two predominant types are the vulnerable type and the grandiose type. The grandiose type is the typical narcissist. They think highly of themselves and display little empathy for others. They are status-oriented, judgmental, and attention-seekers. They constantly criticize others and over-emphasize their own accomplishments. Their accomplishments often do not match their inflated sense of self-worth. They will use and manipulate others, turn people against each other, abuse their spouse and children, cheat on their spouses, and when it no longer becomes possible to control and feed off their partners, they will leave to find another victim. They are fixated on social status and will often go to the courts or your family members to turn others against you because to them, that is the worst imaginable punishment. This type of narcissist may have an actual inability to sense the emotions of others, or if he can, will become angry at the expression of emotion, which he sees as weakness.

The vulnerable narcissist is less stable in his self-worth. He constantly scrambles to prove his greatness, but frequently, sometimes secretly, feels inferior and a powerful sense of shame. This kind of narcissist is desperate for control in his relationships. He will isolate himself and his partner from family and friends to have complete control. He does not want the family to know anything about his personal life because of the threat that he will be ashamed of his spouse, his house, his car, his job, himself. Yet, he feels a great sense of entitlement, especially to the attention of his significant other. In defeat, this type of narcissist will sink into a deep depression and threaten, attempt, or commit suicide.

Narcissists Have Shame-Trauma During Development

Sometimes, the narcissist is not someone else, but ourselves. Narcissists frequently experience anxiety, depression, bipolar mood swings, and other negative emotions in tandem with their desperate pursuit of attention, status, and control. Being a narcissist is not as fun as it may look to outsiders. The narcissist often hides deep feelings of shame, and obscene past traumas such as mental, physical, or sexual abuse. They may have been abused by someone who enjoyed making them feel ashamed and humiliated at themselves. Sometimes, they have had cold and uninvolved parents, who, despite being emotionally absent, were brutally judgmental. These traumas caused them to become fixated on the shame-pride axis. They are severely afraid of being shamed. They will guard their past trauma with their lives. They would rather die than for others to know what happened to them. The narcissist may come from a poor background and become fixated on appearances of financial success they may not be able to afford. They "protest too much" about their worth and status due to deep embarrassment from their past. Sometimes, they will unaccountably avoid a particular family member they grew up with, avoid talking about him, or show rare signs of fear when that person is around. This person may be involved in or know about a trauma that made them who they are. That person is the kryptonite to their armor, making them go immediately from pride to deep shame.

The Development of Lack of Empathy

All narcissists developed differently. Some had no specific trauma. A different type simply lacked empathy, the ability to sense what others were feeling. Because of this inability, he discovered that after being around him for a while, others would predictably flee from him. He experienced this abandonment over and over again as a child, so he became desperate to make people stay. Some of us ran into these types as children, the friend who talked over everyone, was braggadocious, obnoxious, then would admit he will give you anything to not leave, after a few rounds of angry denials that he cares at all. Most children grow out of that, but some don't. Eventually, everyone would figure out there was something wrong with him, keep from his company, and talk behind his back. He would feel shame and anger and wonder why anytime he tried to make a friend, they would run off. However, this experience for whatever reason, could not install the ability for empathy into this individual. He may be biologically incapable of some forms of empathy, an inability that shows up also in Autism spectrum disorders. This type of narcissist, lacking the ability to pick up on the feelings of others, requires constant praise because it is the only way he can tell if someone likes him or is going to leave him. He cannot tell by their tone of voice, facial expressions, or other behaviors because his disorder is such that it causes impairment in this common ability. He finds other ways to make people stay with him, so he learns a sociopathic form of manipulation. He may try to pay them with money and gifts, or try to make them feel guilty or hurt because he has found that these tactics will cause some persons to be stuck to him, not in a relationship of comfort and security, but rather of hurt, fear, and exploitation. This is the only type of relationship he knows. He has not caused himself to be this way; rather, he has a "dis-ease" and "dis-order". For the narcissist who is capable of some form of insight, there is hope of improvement. Symptoms of depression, anxiety, and delusion can be treated pharmacologically, and with counseling. Counseling with social skills training can teach the narcissist to pick up on the feelings of others, even if he can only do this intellectually rather than emotionally. If we ourselves are the narcissist, there is hope of improvement or recovery.

Criteria for a Personality Disorder

Here are the DSM-5 general criteria for a personality disorder as of June 2011.

The essential features of a personality disorder are impairments in personality (self and interpersonal) functioning and the presence of pathological personality traits. To diagnose a personality disorder, the following criteria must be met:

1. *Significant impairments in self (identity or self-direction) and interpersonal (empathy or intimacy) functioning.*
2. *One or more pathological personality trait domains or trait facets.*
3. *The impairments in personality functioning and the individual's personality trait expression are relatively stable across time and consistent across situations.*
4. *The impairments in personality functioning and the individual's personality trait expression are not better understood as normative for the individual's developmental stage or sociocultural environment.*

5. *The impairments in personality functioning and the individual's personality trait expression are not solely due to the direct physiological effects of a substance (e.g., a drug of abuse, medication) or a general medical condition (e.g. severe head trauma).*

Technically, narcissism is listed in the Diagnostic and Statistical Manual of Mental Disorders Fifth Edition (DSM-V) as Narcissistic Personality Disorder. A personality disorder has several features. First off, it causes problems in self-functioning, such as self-identity and self-esteem, and it causes problems in relationships. The narcissist is excessively fixated on praise/shame. His ego and self-esteem may be very fragile and easily challenged and he may react vengefully and brutally. The tragedy of a thousand insults and embarrassments in his mind pile on behind the slightest insult and he over-reacts to it. In Edgar Allen Poe's popular short-story, *The Flask of Amontillado*, the main character Montresor, takes revenge on a fellow wine-taster, Fortunato for a slight insult for which he felt enormous shame and anger. He lures him into going into the catacombs for a special flask of wine, but reaches a niche, wherein he chains up his friend Fortunato, then uses brick and mortar to entomb him alive in the catacombs. Montresor is telling this to an unknown listener, bragging as a narcissist is wont to do. He reveals his family coat of arms reads "Nemo me impune lacessit,", meaning "No one attacks me with impunity!" He is a classical narcissist and his coat of arms suggests he comes from a long line of narcissists, a genetic connection which also shows up in the scientific studies, and which will be discussed in the subsequent books of this series.

Secondly, a personality disorder must have pathological traits which are stable, that is, lasting and persisting in various situations. In other words, the narcissist is unable to change over months, years, or in different contexts. He will continue to brag about his accomplishments even to a friend who has suffered a tremendous setback to which a normal person would be sensitive. A friend may lose his job, for example, and tell the narcissist. Instead of comforting him, the narcissist will brag about his superior qualities and how he would never lose a job because he is so much greater than his friend. He will cut in and talk over the grieving buddy. He may even have disdain for him in his time of need. Such actions are inappropriate to the situation, but the narcissist is unable to sense the emotional and interpersonal context and respond appropriately. The narcissist will be this way for many years. However, young males are more likely to be narcissists, which suggest that narcissistic traits may decrease with age, as testosterone and other biological status-driven hormones become tempered, and experience teaches humility. But there could be other reasons for a lower diagnosis rate, such as that older narcissists have already been diagnosed or are less likely to seek or be forced into treatment. Narcissism is often discovered during treatment for a comorbid disorder like stress or depression, as narcissists are unlikely to think their personality is problematic itself.

Narcissistic traits must not be appropriate to the person's age or environment for diagnosis. Children are likely to behave in selfish ways during development, this is not narcissism. Nor is the focus on rugged individualism and rational selfishness in western cultures. For diagnosis, the pathological traits may not be the effect of drug abuse, such as the psychotic grandiosity produced by amphetamine, cocaine, and sometimes opiates. It must not be the result of a medical condition such as head-trauma or an adrenaline-producing tumor. The famous case of Phineas Gage comes to mind. During a construction job, Gage was accidentally struck in the head with a metal pole propelled by an explosion. The subsequent frontal lobe damage caused him to behave in an uncontrolled and selfish manner. This is not narcissism due to his behavior being the result of a traumatic brain injury.

Criteria for Narcissistic Personality Disorder

Here are the DSM-5 criteria for narcissistic personality disorder.

The essential features of a personality disorder are impairments in personality (self and interpersonal) functioning and the presence of pathological personality traits. To diagnose narcissistic personality disorder, the following criteria must be met.

> A. *Significant impairments in personality functioning manifest by:*
>> a. *Impairments in self-functioning (i or ii)*
>>> i. *Identity: Excessive reference to others for self-definition and self-esteem regulation; exaggerated self-appraisal may be inflated or deflated, or vacillate between extremes; emotional regulation mirrors fluctuations in self-esteem.*
>>> ii. *Self-direction: Goal-setting is based on gaining approval from others; personal standards are unreasonably high in order to see oneself as*

exceptional, or too low based on a sense of entitlement; often unaware or own motivations.

b. Impairments in interpersonal functioning (i or ii):

    i. Empathy: Impaired ability to recognize or identify with the feelings and needs of others; excessively attuned to reactions of others, but only if perceived as relevant to self; over- or underestimate of own effect on others.

    ii. Intimacy: relationships largely superficial and exist to serve self-esteem regulation; mutually constrained by the little genuine interest in other's experiences and predominance of a need for personal gain

B. Pathological personality traits in the following domain:

  a. Antagonism, characterized by:

    i. Grandiosity: Feelings of entitlement, either overt or covert; self-centeredness; firmly holding to the belief that one is better than others; condescending towards others.

    ii. Attention seeking: Excessive attempts to attract and be the focus of the attention of others; admiration seeking.

C. The impairments in personality functioning and the individual's personality trait expression are relatively stable across time and consistent across situations.

D. The impairments in personality functioning and the individual's personality trait expression are not better *understood as normative for the individual's development stage or socio-cultural environment.*

E. *The impairments in personality functioning and the individual's personality trait expression are not solely due to the direct physiological effects of a substance (e.g., a drug of abuse, medication) or a general medical condition (e.g., sever head trauma).*

For a diagnosis of Narcissistic Personality Disorder, there must be impairment in personality function with regard to identity or self-direction. The narcissist has an excessive focus on appraising his value. He/she may think or say he is the smartest person in the world or the best-looking person in the world. At school, work, or hobbies, she will tie her self-worth to performance and competition. He/she may as a side effect convince others of his abilities, giving them also unrealistic expectations of what he can do. His self-esteem may go back and forth between extreme highs and severe lows. He may go from bragging about his looks to asking frequently if his collar is out of place, his belly bulging, and his hair done right. The narcissist goes from feeling on top of the world from a slight gain in income to feeling like an abject failure from a slight loss, even if he is still very well-off. Losing a job can send him into a depressive or suicidal tailspin, going from feeling superior to feeling like he has always been an imposter and an inept failure. He may extend his low self-esteem to his significant other, thinking anyone who would love him after his failure must be the only person on earth more pitiful than himself.

The narcissist will set goals which are too high or too low. He may have a skill, such as baseball, and think he must have been the best in the world at it when he is merely average and failed to advance to high-level teams. He will rationalize his failure or insist he didn't want to make the team. He may think he is the smartest person in the world, despite lackluster educational achievements and incompetence at decision-making. The narcissist may have delusional goals such as being the President of the United States, a governor, or at the top of whatever field he is in, despite being merely average or sometimes below average in ability. Even where he has significant talent, his goals will be unrealistic. The narc may continually make and drop plans to associate himself with those at the highest levels of fields in which he is at the bottom. He may attempt to contact Bill Gates if he has an idea for a computer program, even though he himself is not a programmer. He/she may be under the delusion that his ideas are acts of genius when they are just unrealistic plans he is not talented enough to carry out. He/she will say he has a cure, an invention, an insight that is going to change the world and be his revenge on anyone who has ever doubted him. As time goes by with lackluster achievements, he will double down on his denial rather than adjusting his goals appropriately.

The narcissist has impairments in empathy and intimacy. As mentioned before, he may be incapable of picking up on social cues and try to compensate by constantly trying to elicit praise. He is insensitive to the emotional hurts others are experiencing and unconcerned with them when identified. He may even have disdain for those experiencing moments of pain.

The narcissist may also be incapable of genuine intimacy. He may select either trophy wives or husbands or a narcissistic 'supply' wife/husband from whom he can seek the praise and admiration he needs. The trophy wife is for show and may be younger, have little in common with the narcissist, and treated as property. His sexual expressions may revolve around humiliation and revenge rather than intimacy and empathy. The supply wife is used to supply attention, constant praise, and to inflate his sense of importance. He wants always to be the most important thing in her life, and will even become jealous at the attention given to their children. He will feel cheated and angered if attention is spent on anyone or anything else. He will therefore often insist his wife not work or go to school as he does not want her attention diverted from him, nor does he want her to gain status and independence from him as this would threaten his sense of importance. The narcissistic husband will isolate his wife. He may be insensitive to non-verbal expressions of affection and therefore treat sex as a competition to impress or opportunity to humiliate. The female narcissist will constantly project her fluctuating self-esteem onto her husband, alternately praising him or brutally belittling him.

How to Disarm the Narcissist

Many persons who seek out information online about narcissism do so due to having been hurt by those with narcissistic traits in their relationships. Often, the relationship has finally come apart after long years of suffering. The narcissist, having been rejected, lashes out with overpowering rage and fury. She/he will try anything to get revenge, from using the children as pawns to lying to authorities that you are an unfit parent, even as far as suicide or homicide. It is important to know that the narcissist is suffering intense pain, though they may try to hide it. She/he will go into high gear attempting to manipulate you, endangering anything mental or physical to which you may be attached. So, what do we do? How do we disarm the narcissist? Here are a few approaches:

Detach from the past, practice mindfulness of the present

It is imperative that you mentally prepare yourself for what will hopefully be a successful and permanent break from the narcissist. You will be confused and your mind twisted with all kinds of concerns: *What school will the kids go to? What will our parents think about the divorce? What will the church think? What will strangers think? I will be a loser. I can't handle life on my own, my narcissist is right about that. He abuses me, but at least he pays attention to me, no one else does. Will anyone ever love me again?*

The narcissist may genuinely love you, or he may be incapable of loving anyone. Each person is different. The narcissist has encouraged these doubts in you, and they are not all irrelevant. But there is something deep within you that knows it is over. Once the relationship is over, you can either let it die completely or let it be tortured to death. Sometimes a relationship which was over long ago can take 10 years and PTSD trauma before a clean break is made. The relationship must be allowed to pass in your mind, you must relinquish attachment to the need for closure from the narcissist. You will never get closure from the narcissist. That would be relinquishing his power over you. You may ask *why me? Why did she treat me this way? There must be something wrong with me, just like she says.*

The simple answer is that, like everyone else, you needed love, attention, and affection. Instead of giving it freely, the narcissist uses it for manipulation, his supply, to get the adoration and feeling of superiority that he needs. He will dangle it just out of reach. Maybe, you never got it from your father. Never had acceptance and unconditional love. So, you seek it from another dominating male, but only one who doesn't give it freely. You may have been turned off by guys who overflowed with adoration and appreciation for you because it was foreign, seemed dishonest, and like you didn't deserve it as you had not earned it. Along comes the narcissist, not afraid to sound obnoxious, and not overly impressed

16

by you. He is a challenge, mysterious, and you have a desire to try to impress him, to gain his acceptance. And though those traits may have been exciting in the beginning, you didn't imagine that after you had had a solid relationship for many years, he would still be acting this way. Remember our diagnostic criteria? The narcissist will continue to withhold praise and affection even after you have done everything in your power to please him. He will suck up and thrive from your frustrations. Your pain is the sweetest nectar to him.

To detach from him, you must recognize him for what he is, a person who cannot give affection and unconditional love. He simply does not have the ability. So, you must leave him where he is, as he is. In your mind, you have to put the issue to rest. And that will bring you to the next stage.

Shut off The Depressive Thoughts: the Default Mode Network

How do you put emotional baggage to rest? Let's look at it this way, the mind has 3 working modes:

1. Past memory,

2. Present functioning, and

3. Learning new things.

When you are ruminating on past memory, this is called the default mode network. The default mode network is a system of brain regions which are active during depressive rumination, thinking about the past, talking with others, tracking their eyes, and other emotional type behavior. It is related to tonic-immobilization in animals and stress immobilization, like a deer in the headlights (eyes wide, can't move). It is theorized this system evolved to handle severely stressful situations in animals, then evolved with humans into a system for dealing with our social environment, essentially in a state of hypnosis as we talk to each other and think about social content. For that reason, when we ruminate on depressive situations and on the past, our response hormonally and emotionally is like that of a deer in the headlights. So, as we are thinking about how to put the emotional baggage to rest, it appears that we cannot do it without bringing up and strengthening bad memories. So, we must focus on our present functioning, and learn new things. This is a technique called mindfulness. It means to focus all your attention on the here and now. Notice new things and build new memories rather than ruminating on the past. In therapy, we can stay active and deal with pass trauma if we are sharing with the therapist and allowing our bad memories to be paired with the safe environment the therapist provides. So traditional therapy and mindfulness can bring us out of the baggage of the past if we stay actively engaged and learning. No amount of ruminating on the past alone will bring us out of it. Our minds are like a box. We don't get to choose what will go into it, what we will experience, especially as children, but we can choose what we will focus on. The things we focus on will become more and more active and the things we leave alone will dust, rust, and fade away. Instead, we can put new things into our box, and focus on the activity at hand, rather than focusing on the things already in the box. The box is the brain, and the things we put in it is our experience. The more you access a memory, the stronger it becomes, that's why we memorize by repetition. To forget something, you have to put it to rest, then let it pass. This doesn't mean to ignore it. When it comes up, recognize what it is, just an activity of the mind out of our control, and allow it to pass without attaching further meaning to it and keeping it alive. When something reminds you of your narcissist, just see that this is one of the many things in your box, and let the thoughts pass. Concentrate on the present moment and experience, even if it's washing dishes or cooking. We look at Martha Stewart cook and it's the most interesting thing to watch, but when we get to do it ourselves, we are the whole time thinking of the worst things which have ever happened to us. The difference is that when we are seeing her, we are engaged in tracking what she is doing. But, when we are doing it ourselves, we are behaving automatically, and our minds are wandering in the land of the lost past.

We have discussed getting therapy and practicing mindfulness to let go of the baggage the narcissist has given us. Let's also be open to the idea of taking prescribed medications like antidepressants and antianxiety agents which can also break the chains of the default mode network, replaying the past, and make us more focused on action and the moment. Engaging activities like exercise and video games can also put us in the flow which gets us out of the default mode network or worry mode.

I recommend Jon Kabat-Zinn's audiobook *Full Catastrophe Living* and his mindfulness audiotapes for a beginner's treatment on mindfulness. Mindfulness lets you know that right now is life. There may be no great joy and no great physical pain. If there is not, this is as good as life gets. Intense highs and lows will come, but this very moment is free and full of possibilities. It is right here where we will spend most of our lives so let's value these moments. Notice your breathing, what these words look like on the page, your connection to me as I am writing these words, the sounds surrounding you as you read. You are comprehending my words but do not disagree or agree, just listen to my voice in your minds' eye. If thoughts come up, the default mode network of the past interferes, just notice your brain, doing what it will do, watch it and let it pass without feeling you have won or lost. These goal posts, starting, beginning, winning, ending and losing are artificial constraints which we put on our thoughts, dividing us up in time when time and thought are timeless and infinite. If you have followed these few instructions, you have just had a lesson in mindfulness. Years of practice will make it no different. This is what it is. It is to pay attention to your current life, rather than ruminating on the past or the false future. Our thoughts of the future are a result of our old mind which contains nothing but the past. So, when we think of the future, we are really thinking of the past. Only when we pay attention to now are we fully present in our lives. This is the strongest way to disarm the narcissist when you realize that you have a life that has everything you need to be happy. You don't need anyone's approval, and you don't need the tortures the narcissist brings.

Let Go of the Bully of Comparison

The narcissist has likely trapped you, as she has trapped herself, with comparisons. She compares you to others, belittling you, saying who is prettier, that you need to lose weight, that you don't make enough money. The narcissist claims to think highly of herself but is also tortured with comparison and defensiveness against those who make her feel low. We also compare ourselves to our past selves, how we used to be: younger, more fit, more active in our thinking, and healthier. The great thing about the past is that it is gone. Comparison is just a thought algorithm (a function in a computer program) that we have learned. It is not an absolute truth and we don't have to use it when it is hurtful to us. Everyone is their own person, there is no such thing as someone being better than another. Your past self is no more. Your 8-year-old self is more similar to some present random 8-year-old than it is to your 25-year-old self. When you see a group of frogs, even if one has a broken leg, you don't say that the other frogs are 'better' than that one. Hierarchies are in the minds of animals, and humans can accept or reject that kind of thinking. So, we can use comparison to see what may be possible for us, but cease using it when it causes pain. When we reach the point of death or near death, it is revealed to us that all the comparison we ever cared about is mute, never should we have let it unsettle us because we all end up in the same place. If we walk away from that near-death experience (as I have), sometimes we can take that lesson with us for the rest of our lives. Life is too short to live for comparisons. Any moment you have physical comfort and security (just for now, not for all time), that is your own paradise. Life won't get better than this with a new job or a trip to France.

The narcissist is tortured by comparison and for years he may have controlled you with it. If you have some sense of wanting revenge, do it by leaving him alone in his own hell, and making your way to freedom from comparison. Turn the urge for revenge into something good, then let it fade away.

Gray rocking the narcissist

Now that you have been to therapy and you've let go of your baggage and of comparison though mindfulness, it may not yet be possible for you to make a clean break from the narcissist, which will be your final goal. He may have partial custody of the kids or be a family member. So, how do you deal with him in a way that will cause him to leave you alone? This is where the method of gray rocking comes in handy. The basic idea is to make yourself uninteresting to the narcissist so that he learns that he cannot get his supply from you. This may be difficult if the narcissist has known you for a long time and knows how to push your buttons, so it may require actual change on your part. You will have to learn how to not respond emotionally to his prodding, rather than pretending not to respond. Firstly, avoid situations where there will be an opportunity for the narcissist to talk to you, like watching TV together, or lingering when picking up the kids. Don't respond to unnecessary text messages or phone calls. Answer any substantive questions posed literally and clearly, and either ignore emotional questions or answer with 'I don't know'.

For example:

Narcissist: "What time do I pick up the kids?"

You: "3 pm."

Narcissist: "Did you ever even love me."

You: "I will see you at 3. Thank you. I want you to have a nice evening." (hang up)

The narcissist will envy and threaten anything you have of value or of which you are sensitive. If you are sensitive about your looks and love your mother, she will say you're too fat for her and your mother hates you, anything at all so that you will go back to her for comfort and reassurance. At last, when you attempt to leave the relationship with an unstable narcissist, violence can be the result so it's imperative to do so safely, which we will explore in detail in the final book of this series. There are also cases where narcissistic males who have never been violent lash out with severe consequences when their partners threaten to leave. This is called the narcissist rage and withdrawal. Like a cat, the narc will strike quickly, and just as quickly flee to safety and denial. Narcissistic women who have been violent in the past can also present a deadly hazard to a partner who attempts to leave. Their entire self-concept of being ultimately lovable is yielding to their worse fear, that they are not loveable. Even if you tell that you love them but it's just not working, all they can hear is that you don't love them, you want to embarrass them, and don't care if they die. They feel intense fear, anger, shame, embarrassment, and betrayal. They cannot be consoled. We have sometimes observed the narcissistic phenotype in the small babe whose mother leaves for only a second to go to the bathroom, he cries until she comes back. But when she tries to hold him again he reacts with anger and gives her an earful until he runs out of tears. A child with a normal attachment will quickly cease crying, but the child with the narcissistic phenotype in his childhood cannot be consoled. His attachment is unstable. The sting of betrayal can't be erased for him. He may even grab a handful of hair and pull with all his baby strength. Some such phenotypes are the same way in adulthood. For biological, developmental, and social reasons, the sting of betrayal doesn't go away quickly, it continues stimulating the brain for hours on end, day after day. For some, this can be explained by having a gene for low production of monoamine oxidase, a brain chemical which degrades noradrenaline when the stimulus stops. When a child has low levels, the brain form of adrenaline does not quickly clear out but leaves him in a fight or flight stage for a much longer time than usual. For this and other biological causes, we can feel both compassion and pity as well as make self-protective negative judgments if we must. For, even if the narcissist cannot help his neurochemistry, the things he may do in response to these feelings are sometimes the very definition of evil.

My Story

From the age of 22 to 27, I was dating a narcissistic personality, with borderline personality features. If I failed to hug her sufficiently on coming from work, she would hold an intense grudge which once came out in violence. We were sitting at the table having dinner. And she accused me first of giving her only a quick hug at the door upon returning from work. When I gave excuses and tried to downplay the situation, she went to the kitchen and got a sharp steak knife. I assured her she would calm down and not use it. Never dare a narcissist. Their whole world is about trying to prove themselves. She came at me with the knife and stabbed my hand. I was able finally to catch her hand, and grab the knife from her. This wasn't the last incidence. Later, upon me standing up to her for her abuse, she grabbed a gun, intent either on shooting me or making me perform acts of humiliation. I was able to disarm her, and twice called the police to help me move out. Yet I returned to her a few times for the sake of the children, and I used the gray rock method. I made myself uninteresting. I made her think I was dating no one because no one wanted me. I downplayed anything that might stoke her envy. I did not dress well when I visited her. I didn't tell her of my accomplishments, did not engage in arguments, and did not tell her when I knew she was lying. I also did not make demands about seeing the children, I pretended to find it a chore, that way she would demand that I come see them. If I had let her know it was my greatest joy, she would have barred me from the house and only let me visit in exchange for money or acts of humiliation. This was my way of gray rocking, appearing uninteresting and valueless to the narcissist so that she can't get her kicks from me. Eventually, she lost interest in attempting to draw her supply from me.

No Contact

No contact is just what it sounds like and it is what you must eventually accomplish regarding the narcissistic personality. It means to have absolutely no contact in person or through media with the narcissist, sociopath, or stalker. This is absolutely the best method as far as results. As soon as you can make a clean break with the narcissist, leave and never look back. This may mean you have to move to a new location. If that is the case, be sure you bring family or move to a place where you have supportive friends and family. Studies show that moving is one of the most stressful things a person can do so be sure you don't move to a place where you fall into isolation and depression. Even if there are lots of people around, if you don't have connections to them, you will feel as if you were on a deserted island all alone. Though you have no contact with the narcissist, you may have love for him. For the sake of your own mental health, you may need to maintain love for those who have wronged you. They have acted the way they have out of ignorance, lack of control, or under the influence of bad experiences from their past. So, we can forgive them, so long as we can keep away and not become victims of their demons.

Questions:

Here are some questions those who have been hurt by a narcissist may ask. Here we will give a short answer but they will be discussed in depth in the coming books:

Why did the narcissist choose me?

The narcissist chose you because you seemed to him like a person he could manipulate, besides being beautiful and otherwise attractive. You seemed to have genuine empathy that he can use against you. You seemed like the kind of person who would feel guilty about having done wrong. Since the narcissist feels little guilt, he can guilt trip you into doing what he wants. He gets his kicks from seeing you confused and in pain. It makes him feel special and wanted.

What did I do wrong?

You stayed with him after he had transgressed your values mentally and physically. You did so out of a need for love, self-esteem, and unity, so there is no blame at all. But you will have learned a lesson so that this doesn't happen to you again in your next relationship.

What to do if I find myself as a trophy or supply wife/husband?

If you find that you are a trophy or supply wife, use the tactic of gray rock until you can divorce and command no contact. You may be able to get a no-contact restraining order. But also be cognizant of the narcissist's hidden feelings. He feels pain, so treat him with respect, but he has a malignant illness of the personality which is harmful to others and you must quarantine yourself from him.

Who is an example of a recent narcissist in politics?

Narcissists abound in politics. A recent example is John Edwards, former Senator from North Carolina. He was having an affair with another woman while his wife was dying of cancer. He was also saying condescending things about his own constituents and others. He himself used the word 'narcissism' to describe his actions. First, he lied about the affair, then fought tooth and nail not to be held accountable. Hopefully, he got a dose of humble pie that will improve his life. There are many other narcissists in the political sphere; the most obvious ones we will save for future e-books.

The effects of narcissistic abuse

"The good news is that there is hope, that love and happiness are real, and it belongs to us."

Abuse can leave us feeling alone, incompetent, humiliated and violated; having forgotten our special privilege of being born of love and to love. Experiences we have had with the narcissist may have sucked the prospect of love and happiness from our minds. The good news is that there is hope, that love and happiness are real, and it belongs to us. We need but recognize it in the innocence of a morning dew drop or the soft trickle of rain on a quiet night. A night like many other nights, and a rain like many other rains, but special as it and we are having our moment of communion, and it is eternal. This is where happiness lies.

Narcissistic abuse can take our focus away from the wonder of the moment, running circles in our heads about what should have been. *Are we good enough? Did we do the right things?* The whole treadmill of guilt and regret. We have sustained psychic and neurological injury in our connection to this damaged and pitiable individual. Our brains may have changed to one of depression or anger. How do we recover?

"In order for the mind to recover, the brain and body have to recover."

Recovering from Abuse Physically

The Exercise Theory of Mental Recovery

The exercise theory of mental recovery suggests that the brain cells are like muscle cells in many ways. The way you exercise, or not, determines how you will move and grow. The same is true for the brain. Brain cells that get used grow, and those that don't wither. Similarly, initial training effects, take 3 to 6 weeks of a dedicated exercise program, and permanent changes in body composition and functioning take about 6 months. The same effect is seen in mind training. It will take about 3 to 6 weeks to get a hold on a new skill and 6 months for those skills to become permanent.

For the mind to recover, the brain and body have to recover. Mental injury causes shrinkage of the hippocampus, it causes harmful hormonal changes and may cause one to neglect one's health outwardly. So, the injury is not just mental it is physical. We first need to rehabilitate the physical part of the injury through diet and exercise.

"THE KEY TO RECOVERY FROM PSYCHIC INJURY IS NEUROPLASTICITY, THIS IS WHEN THE BRAIN GROWS AND CHANGES."

Neuroplasticity

The key to recovery from psychic injury is neuroplasticity, this is when the brain grows and changes. The adult brain was once thought to be fixed, but it was later learned that the brain remains able to change throughout life, it merely becomes fixed in some persons due to patterns of living in the past rather than having new and challenging experiences. The programming of the narcissist sends the mind into a loop of shame, guilt, and blame, pumping out harmful stress hormones and shrinking the brain. To get the brain back to peak health, we first must prime it physically with mindfulness, diet, and exercise.

The power of will is overstated. We are all biological animals which respond to our genes and environment. While motivation is the spark of change, it will not itself cause change. Change is physical. We must literally change the brain cells, and this requires cues from our environment, behavior, and our bodies. Your skin won't tan just because you are really motivated to get a tan, you must seek out an environment that provides the amount of sun for the right amount of time to tan. The same occurs with the changes in the brain created by the narcissist. To change, you have to seek out a supportive environment and work out your brain muscles in that environment for at least 6 months (remember the 6-month rule).

"THE KEY TO CHANGE IS ENVIRONMENTAL ENRICHMENT."

Environmental Enrichment

The key to change is environmental enrichment. The most obvious step is to remove the narcissist from your environment and to have family and friends close by and to be involved in your community to whatever extent is possible. If you don't have access to very many people, this can mean taking care of animals and a garden. It is important, to whatever extent you can, to go back to getting meaning from the bounty of the earth, the plants, and animals that surround you. If you are disabled, you might get a service dog. There are many ways to enrich your environment. It is important to install exercise equipment. I recommend a treadmill desk for those who work on a computer and eating a variety of healthy foods. Diet and exercise are the most important components of physical and mental change.

Studies of animals raised in enriched environments reveal 25% more synapses than controls. They have much more brain growth and change. To change, the brain must grow, just like the muscles. Most of this change is accounted for by exercise alone.

you need about 25 minutes a day of aerobic exercise, be it walking, running, cycling, or treadmill exercise.

Exercise

Brain growth must be set off by exercise. Studies show that dancing, especially with a group, causes the most brain growth of any other exercise because it combines exercise, socializing, mental work, and sometimes physical contact. Physical contact is important for all human beings. Like other primates, we groom each other to release endorphins, oxytocin, and to initiate bonding. When stressed, it is a good idea to set aside time to get a massage from a trusted family member or a professional.

As far as exercise goes, you need about 25 minutes a day of aerobic exercise, be it walking, running, cycling, or treadmill exercise. For more quick exercise tips, see Stefan Cain's Amazon book *Essential Time Hacks* for a list of quick exercise routines.

The Neuroplasticity Diet

To get your mind back on the path of love and happiness, you have to feed it the resources it needs to be healthy and to transform. Studies indicate that many different methods of fasting and dieting induce neuroplasticity, or the ability of the brain to change. Here is a list of some of the most effective:

1. Intermittent Fasting
2. The Mediterranean Diet with only black decaf coffee for breakfast
3. Reduced Carb Diets
4. The Caloric Restriction with Optimal Nutrition Diet (CRON)

It is important to thoroughly research each diet and follow them responsibly to avoid negative side effects and make sure they are a sustainable fit for you. Another, easier to remember approach is to simply remove all white grains, sweets, breads, rice, and processed sugars like sodas from your diet, and eat only fresh, unprocessed meats, fruit, and vegetables from the fresh produce section. You will feel better immediately and your health will improve. And according to our six-month rule, your gains in mental and physical health will become permanent. A quick overview of these diets can be found on Amazon in Stefan Cain's e-book called *Essential Time Hacks*.

"AVOID THE TRAP OF COMPARISON."

The Trap of Cry Now, Laugh Later

One of the causes of our depression is that, because we are so focused on the problems in our minds, put there by years of abuse, from parents, spouses, bullies, and narcissists, we are simply not taking care of ourselves physically. We may be unmindful that we are sitting in a painful position, we are taking short, panting breaths, we are hungry and ignoring it or have overeaten to self-medicate, and we have let our appearance and the appearance of our belongings become rough, causing others to worry about us. Conversely, we may have dedicated our lives to a punishing work routine that is hurdling us toward a stress-related heart attack. We think that by ignoring our present needs and present moods, we will accomplish something that will make us happy in the future. However, that is not how happiness works. Happiness is simply having peace in the moment. It is not pleasure, nor pain. It's mere peace in this very moment and it is abundantly available to most of us. Even those of us currently in intense pain, may yet be able to find it in moments of relief, no matter how brief. Our tendency to try to sum up all our experiences of life, then say whether we are happy or not is just a trick we have learned from our social environment. It is a word and words are technologies, not realities. Happiness can never be in the past or future, it can only be had right now, and only if we allow it.

The narcissist has trained you in the 'carrot before the donkey' form of happiness, as something always just out of reach, which you are not deserving enough to have, and only scraps of which can be gotten from the narcissist. He may himself believe in this form of happiness, and thus be himself miserable. Every life is full of ups and downs, joy and suffering. Any life can be summed up as happy or unhappy if we compare our present life to our past selves or to others. We can avoid the trap of comparison. In comparison to other people's lives, ours may have been horrendous, but we can't live anyone else's life, so there's no point in comparing when it comes to our happiness. In Albert Camus's *The Stranger*, the main character, rightly or wrongly imprisoned for murder, muses that he might be well satisfied for the rest of his life, just naming the objects in his small prison cell, or living in a hollowed-out tree trunk. And one might, except for the sting of comparison. Comparing oneself to how others are living, or to how you once lived.

"Our narcissist is a damaged individual, and he has thrown himself in competition with everyone and everything in the world."

Undoing the Damage

"So, in our mindfulness, let us practice non-judgment. We will then find peace, and soon, if we practice daily, it will become a permanent part of our personality and we cannot be touched by the narcissist."

Now that our minds are physically unlocked, the real work can begin. We must undo the programming that the narcissist has carefully and systematically instilled within us. We must deconstruct these malignancies which have been implanted into our brains. The first thing we have to understand is this: words are technologies, not realities.

Let's look at that. What exactly is a technology? It is an algorithm, or a heuristic, a constructed piece of information, either in word form, or physical form, that a human being or other animal has put together to solve a problem. It has a function. All of language is technology, in fact, a technology that most animals do not share with humans, except a few carefully trained gorillas who can do some forms of sign language. First, the narcissist has convinced you that words are a reality. Therefore, he may call you fat, and claim that this is a true reality. However, what is that word as a technology? Is the intention of that word to measure your mass? Of course not. It is not a statement of fact, it is a word which function is to hurt your feelings. To make you feel low. To make you have anger toward him or her, and yet to want to do things to please them so that they will like you. But, it sticks with you because you yourself have learned that these words are reality. In grade school, a child may have called us 'poopoo face' and our little brains couldn't fathom it. We begged him to take it back as if his words could turn us into an actual 'poopoo' face. As we grew up, we may have heard our own kids use that word against others and see the sadness on the face of the innocent believer. The child believes it is something real, and something that makes them less than others. But the grown-up nearly laughs, because obviously there is no such thing as being a 'poopoo' face. Yet, the word has real consequences.

When your narcissist calls you ugly, once again, he is using a technology, a weapon against you, not stating a reality. In the first example, if truly he were pointing out the health consequences of your actual mass, he might offer some suggestions about how to regain peak health, with no hate, no accusation, but that was not his intention. If he calls you ugly, surely there is no attempt to state a reality, the function of the word is simply to make you fall into comparison and feel bad about your looks, though you are a beautiful person. Words are tools, and these words, he is using as a hammer, and it is causing damage to your mind and body. Stress hormones are flowing, brain cells are changing, body cells are aging due to this influence. So, how do we stop this process?

First off, we must stop judging. Can we see all of humanity the same way we see dogs? Aren't they all innocent? Some may have rabies, others may be aggressive because of the environment they came from. Yet, we can love them all, no matter how many cats they have chewed up in their unaccountable aggression. Some we must avoid or encage for the safety of others none-the-less. Can we see humans this way? Blame is a technology, not a reality. It allows us to identify individuals who may be causing harm and take appropriate action which is effective to stop them. But they are not actually evil. Evil is another technology, which allows us to identify those doing harm, and in many cases, to dehumanize them and not care about their lives. So, we should only use this technology in extreme situations, and if we are truly saintly, we don't use it at all. Believing there is evil in the world only causes us fear and harm. There are many harms to avoid and always have been, but it is we who have created this transcendental evil, permeating the universe and the human mind, like a ghost using magical powers to make us miserable. Misery and suffering are just part of life, we need not compound it by making it more powerful than it is with our word technologies. Nor should we use it to dehumanize others. Our narcissist is a damaged individual, and he has thrown himself in competition with everyone and everything in the world. He cannot have peace. And who knows what traumas may have made him that way. We should pity and have compassion for him, but first, we must cut all ties, so that we can work on ourselves. Can we escape the whole of this system of comparison and judgement or must it never end? Must we end our lives, even at a ripe old age, despising our weakened flesh, jealous of the bubbly 20-year-old basking in life's blessings? Surely, we can't take that kind of misery to our graves. So, in our mindfulness, let us practice non-judgment. We will then find peace, and soon, if we practice daily, it will become a permanent part of our personality and we cannot be touched by the narcissist. We will have transcended his childish ego.

We must realize also, that everyone that thinks that words are realities is in a delusion. They are worried about their looks, their appearance of financial stability, their rank. That is a never-ending game of war that ends with us shriveling up into an old cripple and tossed into a nursing home if we haven't taken care to love others so that they love us back in our time of need.

Using Words to Heal Not to Kill

Since words are technologies and not realities, we have to look at what words do. One thing about technologies is that you do indeed have to use the technologies available. There are only so many new words and ways of using them we can invent in our lifetime, and many of us are not skeptical of words and just use our words conventionally. Word use is thought control. We think that we come to our own conclusions about things but the words that we use and accept have the possibilities for each conclusion already built in, so once you accept the word, you accept the conclusion. For example, if someone calls you beautiful, and you believe it as a reality, then certainly as you get old, you may become ugly and

38

believe that too as a reality. Instead, let's look at the intention of the word instead. The person who called you beautiful meant to be kind, hopefully, and it is that sentiment which you want to be mindful of and to respond to. The words themselves are loaded with traps and contradictions, which if you accept, will control you. If you believed you were beautiful as a reality, now the wind is blowing and your hair is becoming disordered and you have lost your composure and your beauty could fade from a gust of wind. Now you are taking hours in the bathroom to get ready in the morning to live up to the concept of beauty which you have accepted. You are being controlled. Some go so far as to get surgery on their precious faces which they should treat with much more care and value.

The things we say have technical content, functions, and emotional content. If someone calls you fat, in western cultures for women, most of the content is an emotional insult. Women of many different sizes have been called that. So, when we encounter negative emotional content, we can have compassion for the speaker. Is the speaker hurt, or insulted by something we did, or jealous of our presence? The best course of action is to protect your mind, by ceasing contact and quickly letting go, but if the person is an important individual in our lives, we must take a deeper approach. We don't have to be hurt because we know that this person is merely using a word technology to harm us out of fear and anger. He is not creating or pointing out a reality. Therefore, we can have compassion. When the dog barks at us, we have compassion. Is he frightened, is he hungry? When the child curses at us, we have compassion, though we may punish to get him on the right path. It is the same with our significant other. But what about the narcissist?

39

It is not our approach to label someone evil or to hate; however, the things we do for those we have compassion for, like the child, and his punishment, is to change his behavior to something that will be more successful for him in the future. The narcissist, unfortunately, cannot change due to his disorder. Therefore, no argument or other action will be effective to change his behavior. Instead, we must use the Grey Rock Method, and the Method of No Contact detailed in Book I of this series.

Therapy

As a therapist with a Master's Degree in Community Counseling, I have dealt face-to-face with the spouses of narcissistic persons. They are generally strong people. Usually, they have gotten entrapped in the fights that the narcissists start and keep running to control them. The narcissist merely wants to feel important. He doesn't care if that importance comes from love or hate. He finds hate elicits more passion and action, so he does things to push your buttons. He says the most awful things he can think of. This can cause anger, anxiety, and depression. It is a good idea to seek individual therapy for these issues, and if you want to keep the relationship together, both partners need individual therapy and group therapy.

Therapy for the Partner of the Narcissist

The partner or other affected victim of the narcissist will need therapy to deal with the mental and physical trauma that went on. There are two ways, informed by our understanding of neurology to deal with these issues. One is to forget them, the other is to deal with them. To forget the issues, you simply recognize that the words said were meaningless, and the things done were out of uncontrolled emotions and bad situations. There is no way to go in and fix them, they are over, and hopefully, you have removed yourself from the situation. You are left with the memories. When you fail to retrieve a memory over time, the mind buries it, forgets it, and it ceases to have strong effects on you. Therefore, if you are not traumatized by an incident, even if it is something that you should have been traumatized by, it's best not to bring it up, or think about it. Let is wither and die. There is a danger that you will re-interprets something that happened to you as a child or adult, and become traumatized by it in therapy where you were not traumatized about it before. So, leave those memories alone, we all have them, and they are best left to die. But, if they are active memories, which are affecting you now, that you need to deal with. Those memories are right at the surface of who you are, how you talk, how you move. A good therapist can see them coming right out of you by how you sit down and make eye contact. How close you sit, your tone of voice, and your effect. He is not probing your secrets, rather, the is becoming emotionally in tune with you so that we can talk like the best of friends, and tell each other anything.

The parts of the trauma which is causing, anxiety, depression, PTSD, insomnia, and constant fear cannot be forgotten. That is the difference. Some things need to be forgotten and not talked about because they were just mixed up situations with no solutions and thank goodness they have passed. But things which are causing symptoms now need to be talked about in a safe environment.

First, pick a therapist you are comfortable with. If you have a choice of therapists, you might ask the head person if you can meet each, talk for a few minutes and pick the therapist you are most comfortable with. Then, after a session, you may want to try a

41

different therapist. It's important to find the therapist that works best for you. In my career, I have found that the most important trait for a therapist to have is simply to be non-judgmental. We are taught in graduate-level classes to provide unconditional positive regard to the client but this does not always happen. Sometimes the therapist has religious beliefs which conflict with your lifestyle. Sometimes they have a punitive mind-frame, especially if they have worked with drug-offending populations. You want to avoid such therapists and find one who is open, who asks more questions to get deeper into the issue instead of just 'telling you what to do." You have your own life and have to make your own decisions and accept the consequences of your decisions. Therefore, you never let a therapist decide for you, because the consequences of that decision will come back to you, and you may not be ready for it. So, make sure you think over any suggestions thoroughly before taking advice.

Once you have picked your therapist, you may take a session to get acquainted and comfortable. It's important the therapist has decent accommodations for you, especially a comfortable chair. Take a relaxing pose in your chair where you can both see the therapist and look away. The therapist will ask, "What brings you in today?" and you will respond either with a short answer or you will write out much of your life story, depending on how comfortable you are. Though the therapist may take notes, everything you say is completely confidential and will never see the light of day. As you are talking to the therapist, a bond will begin to form. It is a bond of friendship and love and that is precisely what it is supposed to be. Sometimes it is mistaken for romantic love, especially when the person has come in due to a divorce or separation. The skillful therapist will know how to handle this situation by making sure the client understands that there has to be distance romantically as we work through the issues for which you sought help. Most therapists have a rule that they cannot date a former client until 2 years after treating them. This is also a law of many licensing boards. However, if feeling develops which hinder therapy, there is the option of choosing another therapist.

Now that you are comfortable, the goal is to face and change the traumatic memories that you have. When you retrieve a memory, the memory changes according to how you feel and think at the time you retrieve it. A study done at the University of Amsterdam with patients with spider phobias was able to delineate how fear memories can be extincted. First, the fear memory must be brought forth. In the 2016 study, Dr. Kindt brought out the dreaded spider. In your therapy session, this can be done by talking deeply about the traumatic memories. At this point, the brain cells for that memory are actively engaged, and the memory is broken up as it's circuits are connecting to other circuits which are active at that moment. Then, Dr. Kindt removed the spider and administered the drug propranolol to the patient. Propranolol is a benign drug, non-narcotic, a beta-blocker used to treat heart pain and in the past, often used by actors to fight stage fright. Once a fear memory is retrieved, broken up, then the stressor removed, it is 'reconsolidated' or put back together, in the hours following the retrieval. Propranolol blocks the process and causes the extinction of the fear memory, with the content memory intact. Patients could then hold or pet the spider without fear. The fear memory was elicited, experienced, but the reconsolidation phase was blocked by the drug. Propranolol is now being studied for use in PTSD.

Those who have been abused by narcissists have traumatic memories which can be treated by the therapist in a similar way. The therapist will first provide an environment of trust, confidentiality, unconditional love, equality, alliance, and friendship for the client. The traumatic memory, be it a beating, or a really hurtful word like "You will never amount to anything, just like your mother!", that memory can be elicited in the safe, therapeutic environment and afterward, during the reconsolidation phase, therapies will be used to relax the patient and to fight the bad thoughts that are elicited by the memory. The reconsolidation phase becomes manipulated and the memory is changed to one which is less threatening. It has been fought and defeated by the client and the therapist and that strength and relaxation become associated with the memory forever. In the future, pharmacological therapies may be used to literally erase the fear memory, without erasing the memory of what happened and this can be very helpful to those who have suffered trauma at the hands of a narcissist.

Summary

In Summary, this is how you recover from abuse from the narcissist.

- Enrich your environment. Enrich your environment with positive cues, pictures, gardening, pets, close friends, hobbies, and install exercise equipment and purchase healthy food.
- Exercise to make the brain plastic. The brain needs exercise to change dramatically.
- Eat a healthy, low carb, natural diet to feed your brain cells.

- After using Grey Rocking and No contact, learn the art of non-judgment of yourself and others. Remember, words are technologies, not realities.
- Pick your therapist wisely and stick to the program.

Questions

Is it possible to have discipline?

Many times, advice is given, and the advice is either good or obvious. But it fails because the listener doesn't have the discipline to carry it out and the advice-giver has left that aspect up to the listener. Sometimes this renders the advice fully impotent. Sometimes, there is not a person on the planet, even the speaker, who has the discipline to carry out the advice. Control your diet, control your eating, control your thinking, we have heard these things before, right? What makes it different this time?

It is this: this time, we are not relying on the will-power of a single person. We are changing our environment. If you want to eat healthy, have no unhealthy food available in your house. If you want to walk on a treadmill, install one in your bedroom and put your computer on it. That way, the only way to use the computer is to get on the treadmill. Also, contact the writer at the email below, your therapist, and others to help hold you accountable for your goals. Once you learn the tricks of environmental manipulation, you will have the keys to change. Also, remember the 6-month rule, it will take 6 months of therapy, diet, mindfulness, and exercise, to cause permanent and lasting change. We will delve further into this aspect in the coming books.

Barry Gray

How to Disarm a Narcissist

Dealing with a narcissist isn't easy. In fact, you feel as if you are playing a constant game of chess where you must be one play ahead of them to successfully counteract their next strategy. You are like the guard dog that is constantly alert and looking out for the signs of potential trouble and conflict.

It's exhausting.

But how am I qualified to describe it as I have above? Well, I like to see it as having been my good fortune, please note the hint of sarcasm here, to have encountered two narcissists in my life. Yes, two of them.

However, I need to stress that the two narcissists are completely different in so many ways, and yet in other ways they are identical. Such are the intricacies of dealing with this kind of personality disorder.

Now, some readers may be wondering what I mean when I say that they are different in so many ways. I can almost hear you say to yourself that all narcissists are the same.

Well, in my experience, that's not the case.

Instead, I'm going to explain why I say they are different, and when I do, you may start to realize that you will then look at the individual that you are dealing with in a different way. It might even make it easier for you to disarm them which is, after all, the entire aim of this book.

The Two Narcissists I deal with

I want you to forget about age or gender or any other physical attributes because that's not important. What's important here are the personalities of the two individuals as that is always going to be the key.

One can best be described as quiet and an introvert. They are more vulnerable, and this shows in their actions and the words that they say, and this is something that became apparent as time went on.

On the other hand, the other narcissist is certainly far more of an extrovert. They are loud, aggressive, and display so many of the common traits of a narcissist in a more open manner.

However, both are narcissists. Both have their own agendas and their own way of trying to manipulate the situation to their advantage. Both can be hurtful in what they say and what they do with us then being left to pick up the pieces as things shatter around us.

Either situation is difficult to deal with from my perspective. I've lost track of the number of times I've felt as if I've been banging my head on the proverbial brick wall attempting to make sense of what is going on. I'm sure so many of you can understand those feelings if you have ever been forced to deal with a narcissist.

49

So, what did I do? How did I move away from that brick wall and start to make progress? The title of this book is how to disarm a narcissist, so it's best I get to my own approach that has certainly made several huge improvements in my life.

A Few Examples of My Situations

To really show how I started to tackle the situations that I found myself in by a different approach, I need to describe those moments. Now, remember that I was dealing with both an introvert and an extrovert at pretty much the same time, so stick with me here.

What I found was that both individuals would 'act up' at various times. They would become aware of a need that they had, which could be driven by several decisive factors, and then the fun and games could begin. Don't get me wrong, when they didn't have any particular need to 'use' me, they would either leave me alone or be that nice person that you always hoped was inside.

But don't be fooled.

That's the problem with a narcissist. They have this ability to come across as being so sweet and innocent, and yet they are merely setting the groundwork for something to come later. You get hooked in, as I did on a crazy number of occasions, and then take control of the situation or get what they want out of it and move on.

Take this for example.

I admit that I try my best to be a helpful person but being helpful was something that would end up causing me more trouble than it was worth. Looking back, I now know that I was allowing myself to be dragged in bit by bit even without my knowledge. Helping here. Helping there. More and more being taken. More and more time was taken up as I was being sucked further in.

But here's the important part. I got to a point where I kind of woke up to what was happening although that then led to another issue, the knowledge that the narcissist in question wouldn't be happy at the change in the status quo.

The result when they found out that I wouldn't help as much? That I had suddenly discovered how to use that massively important word, 'NO'?

Well, for anybody that has dealt, or is dealing, with a narcissist, then it really doesn't take rocket science to work out that they were not best pleased.

As soon as they understood that things had changed, well that's when the fun and games really did begin. You need to keep in mind that when I was basically doing what they wanted me to do like a faithful puppy (albeit a stupid puppy), and they had no need to bring out the horrible side to the narcissist. In short, when I was compliant, I was getting the light and watered-down version of their personality disorder.

That, in their mind, would have to change.

I went from being the compliant individual to being one of the most horrible individuals on the planet. I was subjected to threats, tears, manipulative tactics, the full works, and all because I 'wouldn't do as I was told.' Now, remember that I'm an adult and not a child, so I have that right to stand up to any individual if I don't agree with what was going on.

But then it's at those moments that you really do see the narcissist bringing out the big guns.

All the time when they were effectively grooming me into the role that they wanted me to play, they had become more aware of my own fears and issues but kept quiet. This is often seen as being golden information that will have its own use at some point in the future.

They were aware that I had issues regarding self-esteem and just not being confident. They were aware that I was a shy person and like to keep myself to myself. To me, the thought of misinformation being put out to individuals that knew me was a horrible thing. It was like my worst nightmare, so it was probably obvious that they would then look at using that against me.

That was what brought about the threats of telling others that know me all about things that I had 'apparently' done wrong. These were people that we both knew and the narcissist in question would have been fully aware of how horrible it would make me feel and would send my own anxieties through the roof.

The Education Begins

The idea that education is power is very true when it comes to dealing with a narcissist. For me, the time that I have spent studying what narcissism is and what makes those individuals tick has been so worth my while. As a result, I now feel better placed to stop them in their tracks and block them from being abusive and using me as they see fit.

Educating yourself about this personality disorder is one of the most important steps to take. It gives you such insight, and from that, you will then begin to come to terms with how you need to then reply to them.

Think of it this way.

If you had a child and that child was constantly running around screaming and acting up, what would you do? Would you just accept that this happened and try to deal with it whenever they acted up, or would you look into why they just continue to act that way?

Most people would choose the latter option as it gives them answers as to why the child is acting that way, and they are then better placed to cope with it better than before.

The same approach worked for me and dealing with my narcissists.

I'm not saying you have to become an expert in the disorder. Far from it. However, even just becoming aware of the ins and outs made a huge difference for me.

Suddenly, I could grasp what made them tick. I could grasp what lay behind all the noise and commotion that they create when they are trying to manipulate a situation or get what they want. I was able to see what was coming, although this is mixed in with experiencing their approach, so I was better prepared to deflect and counteract. Also, by being more educated on it all, what they said and did had less of an impact on me than it did before. To me, this was huge, and I'm sure that if you can work yourself into the same position that you will feel the exact same way as I did.

Of course, by reading this book, you have already taken this step. However, I'd suggest that you do as much reading as possible and learn from others that have been in the same situations and see what they did. You will ultimately come up with your own approach that works for you and your circumstances.

Saying that, I do have a few steps that I took, and indeed still take, to deal with the narcissists and their now relatively futile attempts to take control of the situation, and of me.

The Important Steps to Disarming Them That You Need to Take

Here's the thing, I only gave a few examples of the kind of situations that I had to contend with, and I could have gone on and on for page after page.

But that's not why you are reading this. You are reading this in the hope of finding some workable solutions that could make a difference with the problems that you are encountering in your life, and that's perfectly understandable.

However, before I go into that, I need to talk about what I did from my own perspective regarding myself. You see, I'm a firm believer that one of the best ways to disarm them is to start from within. After all, often the narcissist is targeting you because of something that they see within your personality or approach to life that is a weakness and can be exploited. It makes sense for you to, therefore, look inwards before looking outwards.

For me, I had to accept a number of important things about myself. I had to accept that there were times where I was simply not assertive enough and that this could come across as being weak.

There was a certain sense of being tired of dealing with the hassles and troubles that can bc brought into your life as a result of dealing with a narcissist and, once again, that tiredness was a weak point.

Clearly, that could then be exploited, and the entire emotional merry-go-round would start all over again.

Looking inwards at yourself is not easy. I had to take the time to look at the aspects of myself that I was not happy with

Disarming the Narcissist

My hope is that by now you have decided that you too need to look at your own self and to get honest with things. It's not easy, and you might not like what you come across, but it's an essential part of this as it was something that did help me along my way.

However, I now need to move forward and go into more details as to the ways in which I sought to stop the narcissists in their tracks. I'm not saying that you are guaranteed success, but you are probably feeling desperate, and at the end of the road, so anything is worth a shot.

Also, I'm not saying that you should follow the steps in the exact order as I'm describing because what works for me might just need a few tweaks and alterations for others. What I'm really trying to do is to give you some hope with what is often regarded as being a rather desperate and pointless situation.

Step 1: Stop and Think

The first thing that I do is to just stop and think. Reacting immediately without putting any kind of thought into it is useless. By doing so, you only increase the chances of falling into traps and inadvertently doing what the narcissist is hoping for.

I always found that by not rushing into anything and doing that instant reaction, that I was putting myself in a better position to react accordingly. I could react more in line with what I wanted rather than what the narcissist wanted.

If you react immediately, then you are primarily giving control back to the narcissist. This is what they want, so it makes sense that if you can stop this, then they lose some of their power.

I know that this was something that I never completely perfected. However, I'm human, so that's perhaps understandable. The most important thing is that I was very aware of my attempts at just slowing things down and effectively buying myself some time.

Of course, this is something that the narcissist doesn't want. They want to try to catch you off-guard to ultimately take advantage of the situation and get what they want from you. They try to keep the momentum going as it serves their own agenda, so by doing the opposite, you throw them into a tailspin. Often, they have no idea about how to then deal with it so resort to threats and being negative towards you.

I've lost count of the number of times that just slowing things down and thinking about it all has made a huge difference, and I strongly recommend that you do the same.

The Introverted Narcissist

I said earlier that I had to deal with both an introverted narcissist as well as one that was certainly an extrovert and louder in their approach. So, in dealing with the introvert, I would often take this approach regarding this very first step.

First, I would think about the way in which they would expect me to react. As they were often highly anxious, I would be there working out how high their anxiety is at that moment in time. That allowed me to decipher if this was their narcissism or an actual request for help, as there is a difference.

I also had to be aware that by slowing things down I was potentially increasing their anxiety. You need to remember that anxiety can make you do weird and not so wonderful things, and this was no different.

The key with this part was for me to not show my own anxieties as that starts an avalanche of emotion that can then be difficult to stop. Taking a moment and thinking it through, and remembering to breathe, just buys that bit of time to keep your own anxiety in check leading to a better response.

The Extrovert

The extrovert was different. They would be far pushier and potentially forceful especially when they didn't get the answer they were expecting and when they wanted it. They would be loud and brash. Shouting and becoming more abusive in an outward manner. It's easy to end up feeling intimidated when you are the complete opposite as a person.

However, I must stress this point. Do not allow all their shouting and animation to derail you. Do not allow them to quickly take control of things simply because they have got louder and louder.

By taking that all-important moment to think things over, you will often find that they get louder and louder, but you need to stand your ground and have the confidence to do so. At first, you might be like me and only stand my ground for a bit longer than I used to, but the foundations were set, and that gives you hope for the future.

Step 2: Thinking About Their Reasoning

A trick that I would use when attempting to disarm them was to turn the tables and look at getting inside their head and thought processes. After all, they do it to me so why should I not go ahead and do it to them?

OK, I accept that I am not as accomplished as they are at it, but by even just making an attempt at it, I would often discover that I had a better insight behind their words or actions. By effectively studying this time and time again, I was able to start to unpick their reasoning that lay behind everything they were doing. Yes, this didn't always work, but I found that it made it easier for me to reply and answer in a way that was beneficial to me, rather than them.

I found that I could only do this when I applied the first step as I needed that time and space to allow those thoughts and the interpretation of what they are saying or doing. If there was too much noise going on in the background, then I would struggle.

By getting to grips with their thoughts and what they were looking for, it meant that I felt I was able to basically turn the tables slightly by putting the focus back on them. I must stress that, at times, they can think quite quickly and come back with a retort, but if you have been able to come to a conclusion as to what is driving them, then you are certainly better placed to reply in the correct manner.

What I found was that, on most occasions, there would be relatively few driving forces behind their actions. Primarily, they wanted something from me whether that be attention, to do some action, money or whatever. There was an expectation and an inability to understand why I would ever dream of not fulfilling that expectation.

But that's the thing. Over time I was able to get better at identifying it and could then start to build my own deflection ideas or blocks that would stop them from going down that path. However, I would still do it in a nice way to prevent the particularly nasty side from rearing its very ugly head.

The Introvert

Going back to the introvert narcissist, I concluded that there was so much fear attached to what they were saying or doing. Anxiety was seeping through, but then I also had to understand that some of the anxiety could be fake.

Let's face it; a narcissist knows how to push your buttons. If one of those buttons is seeing someone upset and you are known for your empathy, then how do you think they are going to try to manipulate the situation? Clearly, they will use anxiety symptoms to draw you in.

I would try to avoid just reacting to what I saw in front of me and instead look behind this anxiety. I would then ask myself these kinds of questions to help me reach a point where I knew how to approach this situation.

- What are they asking of me?
- How much of their reaction is real?
- What reaction are they expecting from me?

If I can come up with these answers, then it just put me in a better position to respond in the correct manner.

The Extrovert

The extrovert is different. They still had the anxiety, but it would often come across as far more aggressive and pushy. At times, it is difficult to withstand that kind of pressure, but you need to be resolute and defiant.

Once again, I would think of the same questions as those I mentioned above, but as they are louder in their approach, it's harder to really listen to the reasons because of all the noise going on. However, to disarm them effectively, you need to cut through all that noise. For this, I would cut my emotions and, through practice, would hone in on the actual words being said.

Often, I would find that they were basically shouting about the same things just doing so from a different perspective.

Step 3: Carefully Constructing My Response

The one thing that I discovered that both narcissists excelled in was taking advantage of the situation when I reacted too quickly, and with too much emotion. Now, I'm not saying that you should be completely emotionless as that's difficult to do, but just as I said in the first step, you need to slow things down.

In some ways, this is difficult to do since there is a tendency for them to push you and push you even further, so they can pretty much take advantage of the situation and to be in control. So, what's the best way to deal with that?

In my case, I would think back to the previous step and ascertain the reasoning behind their request and to determine what exactly it is that they are asking me to do, or what they want. I would then have to consider that request quickly in my mind to decide if it was reasonable and fair or if it was an attempt at manipulation and to take control of a situation.

If I decided that it was the manipulation aspect, then obviously I couldn't allow that to continue. In those cases, I would do the following.

- Pause for thought.
- Avoid being pushed into an answer at their pace.
- Take a deep breath.
- Assess the reasoning behind their request.
- Determine how I feel about the request.
- Stay calm.

For me, the last part was the most important. I know I'm an emotional person, and let's be honest emotional and empathetic people are very attractive to narcissists. Keeping your emotions in check allows you to keep control of various parts, and this is going to become clear to the narcissist and force them into either moving on elsewhere or changing tactics completely.

Step 4: Show Careful Empathy

Remember that the narcissist is looking for something from you. In my experience, they have believed that everyone has an agenda, which is really them projecting since they themselves are the only people.

This was always a difficult part for me. I was always wary of showing too much empathy and falling into my old ways. That was until I spent some time getting to grips with how to control the empathetic individual inside of me.

It's a fine line that you cannot cross. For me, both narcissists would take as much as they could get even if the door had been left slightly ajar. Give them a hand, and they take not only the arm but that entire side of your body and still want more.

So, here's what I ended up having to do so that I could indeed disarm them and stop them in their tracks.

With my empathetic response, I would usually open a reply by showing a slight hint of it. However, I would then finish the rest of the sentence in a more neutral tone that really set out my response.

Often, they would start to be drawn in to the fact that I was showing some empathy, but then they are stopped in their tracks simply because I was not then doing what they wanted. I put it across in a nice manner, without emotion, and often even offered them some hope in them finding some solution to what their problem was at that time.

Effectively, I would throw the ball back into their court, and the more you do it, then the more they are going to become aware that the ball just keeps on coming back. Dealing with you in this way becomes pointless. You are not feeding them with what they need.

Step 5: Being Assertive and Not Aggressive

The one thing that I eventually discovered was that the narcissist doesn't expect you to be assertive. They do, at times, expect aggression as it can be an indication that they are getting under your skin and can then manipulate that emotion to their advantage.

Trying to be assertive is something that you can learn if it doesn't come naturally. I know that it's an area that I struggled in, so I sought help from a trained specialist who helped me with this part of my personality.

So, what would I do, and how would this disarm them?

You must remember that the narcissists I was dealing with were used to me following the line that they were feeding me. When you then do something that disrupts that, then they will often not know what to do, or will simply start acting out even more.

If you are aware of this, then you can handle it better, but I did find that I couldn't back down. Being assertive in the face of this pressure would involve me sticking to my guns. I would then go on to say things such as:

"I will not...."

"You are asking the wrong person..."

"I refuse to..."

For me, the key part was that there was no ambiguity for them to take advantage of. There was no sense of indecision in my replies, and that's something that you need to do yourself. Any indecision will be leapt upon, and that's not a good position for you to be in.

Also, I would strongly recommend that when you are trying to be assertive with them that there is no quivering in your voice. There must be conviction in what you are saying, or else it becomes pointless. I would work at having a stern tone to my voice to combat this, and it does help when it comes to getting your point across.

Step 6: Understanding My Own Response

One thing that I had to come to terms with was the potential role I could have been playing in continuing to enable the narcissists to carry on as they were. Being an enabler is something that you perhaps don't notice at first but thanks to educating yourself on narcissism and understanding what makes them tick, then you can begin to see that this could very well be a possibility.

Of course, my actions and not just my words were playing an important role. If I look back at my earlier reactions, then I was just doing the same thing over and over again. I would put up some resistance and then cave in when more pressure was being applied.

I looked at my response. I spoke to my CBT therapist to get help to change that response, and then I would seek to answer or handle things in a different manner. This change of approach was then something new for the narcissist to deal with, and it would stop them in their tracks, especially if I was no longer going to be helping them or enabling their situation.

Step 7: Understanding Showing Empathy and When to Stop

It's good to remember that there may be times where the narcissist does need help for something and that it is genuine. You can easily be drawn into this belief that everything is going to be a game or has an agenda, but that's not the case.

To really disarm them, you need to be aware of how to show empathy and when to stop it due to them starting to take advantage of the situation and your response.

For me, I would constantly assess and re-assess the situation depending on their replies. This is something that gets easier the more you do it, and it is tiring mentally, but it's the best way of keeping in control of the situation.

I had to effectively plan ahead, just like the chess game I mentioned at the outset, and to be aware of the line that I wouldn't cross. Also, they are both good at showing fake empathy, so even if you are not feeling particularly empathetic, just showing them it right from the outset and still sticking to your guns with not doing what they want you to do will throw them. It will remove the power that they have had over you.

Just remember not to come across as cold and uncaring as they tend to be. That's not my personality so why should I change it just to suit them?

Important Answers to Disarm the Narcissist.

The final part, or step, which I feel I need to discuss is looking at various answers that I have used to successfully disarm the narcissist that I am dealing with at that time. Now, I'm not saying that these answers are always going to work, but my hope is that it will provide you with your very own sense of inspiration as to what to say at the appropriate time.

I have to admit, that answering the narcissist is going to depend on everything else that I've mentioned above. By the time I've got to the point, especially at the outset when I am learning more about how to handle them, I've worked through my understanding of the situation and whether I want to go down a path.

If not, then I must be ready to give the correct answer, well the correct answer for me, to stop them in their tracks and deflect the attention away from myself.

So, what do I do? Well, I'll give you a few examples of how I was able to learn how to answer them correctly. Clearly, this is only a guide, and the examples that you could give would probably be vastly different, but the same idea and concept remains the same.

Example 1:

"You used to be a caring person, but now you're not.... you've changed"

I've had this said to me on more than one occasion, and at first, it hurts to hear it. However, once you have a better understanding of the entire thing, then you can really see what's behind it.

With this, they were basically saying that I'm no longer a caring person because I'm not doing what they want me to do. There's no concept as to whether I wanted to do it in the first place. There's just an acceptance that surely there could be no way that I wouldn't follow suit and effectively obey their commands.

For this, I would generally answer along the lines of.

"I'm sorry you feel that way about me, but I cannot and will not do that."

What I've done here is that I've kind of opened the answer with a touch of empathy, but then followed it up by a clear statement that my mind has not been changed by their approach. It's always important that I answer this without sounding angry, upset or emotional in any other way as they feed off that. They feed off me being upset about something as it opens the door for me to be manipulated.

66

Example 2:

"I'm going to tell everyone what you are REALLY like."

In this example, the narcissist is looking at trying to take advantage of a weakness that they know I have with my personality. I get anxious around people thanks to a social phobia, so by threatening me with this idea of basically telling people a lot of lies about me, they hope it will scare me into submission.

At first, this kind of line was a tactic that would work until I concluded that people would not really care as much, or even listen, to the extent that I had initially feared. This is a good example of how the work on my own self can pay dividends.

I would tend to reply along the lines of.

"I'm sorry that you feel the need to discuss things with others. I hope they can help you."

With this, I've shown empathy at the start once again, but only in small amounts. I've also then thrown open the door for them to go ahead and tell people because I was aware how their demands and reaction were so far out of the norm that anybody listening would be amazed at how they were reacting.

This was all about not worrying about their potential actions and standing my ground once again. The narcissist that comes out with a threat such as this, where they are trying to take advantage of a perceived weakness, is then disarmed as you have not reacted in the way they were expecting.

Example 3:

"You have never done anything to help me."

This should, in my experiences, be the motto for narcissists. Of course, what they are really saying is that you aren't doing what they want you to do at this moment in time. However, this is a point that is easy to then get drawn into an argument, which they can thrive on especially if you are like me and more of an emotional type of person.

With this, I would first disarm them by not getting drawn into that argument or showing too much emotion. This is that sign of weakness and even if you feel that you want to shout back at them, don't. Trust me when it says it gets worse.

I used to fight back until I got wise to it, and I would be thrown out of their home and would be told I was this horrible person, and at the end of the day, I didn't exactly win by fighting back.

That's why you must be clever and intelligent with your approach. Just flying off the handle no matter how frustrated you may be with the situation is not the way to go. I did that, and then my life was practically made hell as part of my 'punishment' so I learned to change my ways.

Once again, I would answer along these lines.

"I'm sorry that you feel that I have never helped you with anything. I hope you find someone who can help you with whatever it is that you need."

You can see here how I would start with empathy followed by a rather neutral statement and that I basically wish them all the best for the future. I'm not giving them any potential leverage and remaining calm always. The two things that a narcissist is not going to like.

There are a whole host of other examples that I could give, but the main idea here has been to just give you an insight on how I structured my answers when faced with different issues or threats that were being made towards me. Never react in an emotional way. It's like energy to them, so don't provide them with that opportunity as that alone is going to disarm them.

My Final Thoughts on Disarming the Narcissist

Throughout all of this, I've been trying to guide you through the maze that is the mind of the narcissist. Both individuals that I've been dealing with have their own unique mind, and yet behind it, all are the same issues, and that's important for you to remember.

I've found that disarming them is something that gets easier the more I do it. I have no doubt that mistakes have been made in the past, but I'm still here and certainly in a better position with the two of them than I have been in for some considerable period of time.

But here's the thing. When I do feel that I've made a mistake, I don't beat myself up over it. That all on its own becomes a door that is ready to be flung open and the old way of dealing with those narcissistic demands and threats becomes an unwelcome visitor.

For me, I had to become more emotionless when dealing with them. I knew that my emotions, and it's tough when you are that kind of individual by nature, was giving them the leverage that they were after and the options to exploit. By changing that approach, you throw them that curveball and force them into trying to change tactics.

However, when they are constantly being blocked in this way, then they do become tired and will often shift their attention elsewhere.

Look at it this way, as I know it helped me when I did this, of the narcissist being like the child and you are the parent constantly blocking them off from hurting themselves. You gently guide them away from where they want to go and no matter how hard they try for another route, you don't let them.

This is all about putting apparent obstacles in front of them. Obstacles that they see as being too difficult to overcome, so they look elsewhere that has an easier path.

Remember, often it will be the case that they have no desire to deal with their personality issue. They don't see themselves as having a problem. Instead, everyone else has issues and they are above that. This means, that in my experience trying to get them to seek help for the way in which they approach things is pointless. One did so for a short period of time, but you could tell that they were not putting their heart and soul into it. They were doing it as part of a manipulation game, which ultimately backfired.

If I had to sum up my own approaches to disarming the narcissists, then I think that I would say the following.

- Learn about your own self first.
- Understand what your own issues are.
- Understand what makes a narcissist tick.
- Be aware of their agenda and manipulative streak.
- Show empathy but know when to stop.
- Be assertive and not aggressive.

- Be strong in your answers and don't back down.

- Know your limitations and don't go past them.

- Answer in a calm manner and stay neutral when possible.

- Listen to them, make sure they know you are listening, and then answer.

- Never rush into saying anything without thinking it over first.

- Avoid getting into an argument. It doesn't help.

- Be prepared to walk away from a situation to diffuse it.

- Be compassionate, but not someone to be trampled over.

Disarming a narcissist isn't easy but it can be done. It's just a case of you working hard at your own self and dealing with the parts of your personality that they are taking advantage of. By having the strength of conviction regarding your own self, you become a less attractive proposition for the narcissist. If they cannot feed off you, then they will go elsewhere, and that's fine.

I still deal with both narcissists, but they are now better aware than ever before that I'm not going to take their rubbish or attempts to manipulate me. They do still try, but I expect that. They do still push their luck, but I remain steadfast in my responses and confident in what I am doing.

Work at yourself and, as a by-product, you will become better at disarming the narcissist ultimately leading to an easier life for your own self.

Recovery from Narcissistic Abuse

"I only spoke to you because I wanted something."

"I'll tell everyone what you are really like if you don't do what I want."

"You were once a good person, but now you aren't."

"I only ever help you, and you never help me with anything...you are always take, take, take."

To be honest, I could go on and on for page after page of comments and things that have been said to me by a narcissist. Even though I've only given you the absolute highlights, it does provide some basic insight into parts of the abuse that can come from a narcissist. Trust me when I say that it can get worse than those four sayings above, but I'll get into it later.

Any kind of abuse can be difficult to recover from, so it's no surprise that narcissistic abuse also falls into that category. It's horrible to deal with. It's difficult to make sense of it all, but you can with the correct help.

So, how am I able to make such statements as those above?

Purely because I'm speaking from that personal experience at dealing with not just one, but two different narcissists in my life. Yes, I really have been quite fortunate in that respect.

I should point out that even though I'm talking about two individuals, they didn't always share the same characteristics. Indeed, one was quiet, anxious and the vulnerable version whereas the other couldn't be any more different if they tried.

However, the actual type of narcissist that you have to deal with isn't that important. I've found that the abuse that comes from them can be pretty much the same, and the recovery from it is certainly identical.

You see, before I go into the part where I discuss my own recovery from narcissistic abuse, and the methods I had to use, I need to paint a more accurate picture of what was going on. For those that are in the same situation as myself, I'm sure you will sit there nodding your head in agreement as I go through my own personal experience.

But as I'm talking about two individuals with a different modus operandi each, then I'm going to break things up into each person. The reason for this is because I've been forced into taking two different approaches because of the individuals in question. However, I will begin by giving some insight into myself.

Me from My Own Perspective

By nature, I'm a quiet person. I like to see myself as being kind and compassionate and, if I'm being perfectly honest, I'm not assertive enough. Now, I understand if those that are familiar with narcissists have already caught onto the biggest issue I have with this kind of situation.

I've never really had that many close friends and I like to keep my emotions in check as much as possible. In other words, I'm quite an introvert and look inwards at myself on a regular basis.

This is just the way that I've been throughout my life. I didn't grow up in a family that wanted to be the life and soul of the party, so I do accept that a percentage of it would have been my upbringing. However, I do believe that this is just the way I was meant to be, and I'm fine with that to a certain extent.

But here's the problem.

Due to the nature of the narcissist, I'm coming across like the wounded antelope that the lion can just toy with and play with whenever they choose. I'm easy prey, and when you include the way in which narcissists seem to have this insane ability to pick up on your weak points, suddenly this antelope is even more wounded than before.

This isn't an attempt at getting some pity. Instead, it's really setting the scene since so many people that simply don't understand narcissists and the way they work are bemused as to why you just don't walk away from them. I'm really trying to just make it easier for you to get to grips with the way in which they can get their hooks into you, and often without you noticing.

Being Honest with Yourself

To recover from this kind of abuse, you need to understand why you were abused in the first place. There must have been something inside of you that drew in the abuser, in this case, the narcissist, or else they would have just walked on by and moved on to another individual.

The only way you can heal is by looking at your emotions, your mind, your character, and anything else that makes up you as a person. This will be something that I will constantly refer to on a regular basis because it really is that important.

Due to my own issues, this wasn't easy. Admitting your flaws never is, but I thought about it from this perspective. If I didn't deal with my flaws, then I would continue to put myself in front of an abusive individual and, in my rather strange mind, I then deserved to continue to be abused simply because I had done nothing to counteract it.

Yes, I know that might sound strange, but in its own way, it does make a certain degree of sense.

It is impossible to recover from something such as this that is coming from the external if the internal is in its very own turmoil. What is it that makes you so attractive to the narcissist? How could this possibly be counteracted by you? Is it even possible to counteract it?

If you believe it is indeed impossible, then I must tell you that this opinion is a load of rubbish.

Is Recovery Even Possible?

I will get to the abuse part next, but I also feel the need to reassure readers that recovery from this kind of abuse is indeed possible. I'm not saying that it's easy, and the way in which you reach that recovery point will be a very personal journey, but it is possible.

It's as much about your own self and coming to terms with your own flaws and rectifying those since you then become less attractive to the narcissist. They see that those negative things in your personality that they loved so much have vanished. Your purpose to them has changed. Your relationship with them has changed.

That's not to say that your relationship with the narcissist has to then be a bad one, not at all. In fact, in one case I would say that various aspects of the relationship have been far more positive. However, there is always that thought in the back of my mind and the need for me to remain on-guard always. After all, I need to watch that they don't try to kick things off again due to their own needs, so I cannot show any sign of weakness.

Recovery is possible, but it's a long road with a few twists and turns. However, I hope that with the points I'll be making later that your own road will have fewer surprises just waiting around the corner.

The problem with this kind of recovery is that you will often have a real feeling of self-doubt about yourself. Let's face it; you have a narcissist abusing you in your life because of nice qualities that you have that they have then been able to take advantage of.

I know that when I look at my own situation that the kind and empathetic qualities in me are things I wouldn't change just to aid my recovery. Why should I change the nice parts of me just to stop a narcissist from abusing them?

The answer is, I shouldn't. If I did, then the narcissist has effectively won. They have manipulated me into doing something that I, in all honesty, would not wish to do.

For me, I had to get to a space where I had reached the end of my tether. I had to get to the point where it was the end of the road. They say that an

The Abuse

For me, the abuse has come from two different directions forcing me into really looking both left and right repeatedly. It didn't help that I was dealing with both individuals at the same time, so you can imagine how my head was spinning around like some character in a horror movie.

Of course, being in this state of mind makes it easier for the narcissist. Whenever you have no idea as to what you are personally doing or just trying to pacify everyone, then they can strike.

It didn't help that I did have my own issues that effectively set me up for all of this.

The abuse that I faced came in different forms. There would be the manipulation. There would be the hidden agenda. There would be the threats, tears, shouting matches. There would be the comments to make me feel horrible and a lesser person. There would also be the play on my weak points, and that was the most popular approach.

But this was the thing. I never knew when the abuse would occur, and I'm sure you are in the same boat. I never knew how bad it would be or how extensive it would be. This is abusive and is one of the reasons as to why it is so destructive for the individual being abused.

If you find that you are in the same kind of boat, then I'm going to help guide you through the steps that I had to take to get through it and recover from it. I did so by working on several important points. I had successes, and I had failures, but I have got there in the end.

The First Step to Recovery: Getting to Your Breaking Point

I'm aware that so far this has been a bit doom and gloom, but sadly that's a space that so many individuals that are dealing with a narcissist will be familiar with. But let's start to move onto something more positive in nature, the first step to recovery.

In my case, I reached that breaking point. I had heard of others talking about this point before, but I never believed I would get there. Looking back, so much of what I said and believed was nothing more than learned behavior, so it's perhaps no surprise that I had zero faith in ever reaching this stage.

But here's the thing.

We are all human, and unless we are completely devoid of feelings and emotions, it will get to the stage where the narcissist just does that one thing that takes you too far and tips you over the edge.

Now, you could be sitting there with the belief that this is going to be a horrible point to be at. After all, nobody enjoys being tipped over their own individual limits. It's an uncomfortable feeling, and there's every chance you will freak out and not know what to do.

However, I'm going to tell you that this is a brilliant point to be at. Once I reached that point, I knew that things had to change and that my own recovery could begin.

OK, at that stage I had no idea what that recovery would be like, but I could sense some hope, and that's what I'm hoping to deliver to you through this tale.

So, what is this first step that I'm speaking of? Well, it's that point that I just mentioned. It's being aware of that breaking point and knowing that you have come to the end of the line. You cannot go on any further. You cannot allow the abuse to continue.

This understanding is key. Without this, I would still be in the same boat dealing with the same issues and putting up with the constant demands and threats whenever I tried to stand up to them.

Now I don't.

How did I know that I had reached this point? Well, my breaking point will be different from your own, so it's impossible for me to specifically state moments where you will suddenly discover that you have had enough.

For me, it was the discovery that it was making me ill. The pressure that was being heaped on me and the weight of expectation was too much. I was having issues with my blood pressure. I was becoming highly anxious at silly things. I was becoming more and more depressed with so many negative thoughts, many of which were being put into my mind by the narcissists.

My body was effectively telling my mind it was finished.

You may feel that this is rather extreme, and to some, it will be, but the main point I'm making here is that my breaking point was when I just could not do it any longer. I also noticed that the narcissists didn't even notice and, in fact, were acting up more simply because I was unable to do what they wanted or expected of me.

Making that discovery that your health and needs just are not important to them is huge. It was at that point that I knew I was being abused and I had a choice. I could either let it make me very ill indeed, and potentially push me into a breakdown of some sorts, or I could act to stop the abuse and then work through the damage it caused.

Clearly, I took the second option.

The Second Step: Improving My Own Self-Worth

Recovery from any abuse begins from within. I was already aware of my own personal limitations and that these were an area to be exploited. Clearly, it made sense for me to then tackle those limitations as, by stopping them from being an exploitable area, it would remove them as a potential area to be abused by both narcissists.

I'm sure you will be aware of how the narcissist has that ability to apparently see into your soul and what is troubling you. I know that it would freak me out at how they just instinctively knew things when, in fact, it was probably due to them paying attention to various things and storing the information away for the future.

You see, depression and anxiety were keeping me down. A person with no real sense of self-worth is an attractive proposition to the narcissist. They can be bullied and pushed into things that a normal person would question.

So, here's what I did.

First, I knew I had to get my own help. For this, I had to get help from experts to allow me to cope with my own limitations. For too long I had largely suffered from the expectations being placed upon me and the abuse inflicted on me without telling a soul.

I do admit that I ended up being put on medication for depression and started seeing a psychologist, one that focused on CBT. This allowed me to look at my own thought processes and the way I viewed myself as an individual and to really start to get to work on changing the negative mind that was dominant.

Now, I'm not saying that everybody will have to go to see a psychologist to help improve their own self, but I would certainly recommend not doing this all on your own. It's a tough road with a few holes along the way, so knowing you aren't alone is actually a big help.

By turning the attention to myself and allowing myself to grow and develop as a human, it made me less attractive to the narcissist. It makes sense that if you are no longer as attractive, and they are basically forced to look elsewhere.

This was something that took time on my part. If I'm honest, I'm still working on it, but each part gives me the confidence within myself to heal and to become even more aware of what it is that I am looking for. The stronger I become, then the faster I move away from being the victim that they target.

The Third Step to Recovery: Creating the Boundaries

I perfectly understand if you are sitting there wondering what on earth you do when you get to that breaking point. In fact, you may have already reached that point and yet are unsure as to what to do next.

Don't worry, I too was in that situation, and I completely understand how it just seems to be so daunting at that time.

For me, I took the opportunity to just stop for a moment and become aware of the fact that even just by reaching my breaking point that I had made an important change. A line had been crossed, but this time no new line was being drawn by the narcissist. I had to be the one to draw the line on this occasion.

But how do you even go about drawing that line when you are so used to it just being trampled on and scrubbed out whenever the narcissist felt like it?

The answer for me was in creating boundaries.

Now, I'm sitting here, and I know that people reading this will be shouting back at me saying that they have tried this time and time again, but the narcissist just walks over them. Alternatively, you have grown tired of scoring that line in the sand only for them to wipe it out with their foot and just proceed.

It's so frustrating, but then I would find that my own line in the sand was relatively weak. It was more like a faint trace rather than anything else. Hardly a difficult or frustrating obstacle for the narcissist in question to then overcome.

This meant that I had to learn more about the boundary creation aspect. I felt that I understood how to do them, but then concluded that in the face of a narcissist, I really had no idea.

So, how did I do it? How did I go ahead and create those boundaries and then have the strength and conviction within myself to police them?

The answer is in getting professional help to do so. This was something that I really did have to learn, but there's no way you can ever hope to recover from the abuse when the correct things are not in place to help you.

The help that I received came in the form of a therapist and counselor, but one that had previous experience in dealing with narcissistic and antisocial personalities. Their experience and knowledge helped a great deal. They knew the answers to all my questions and made me understand that I'm not the first person to have been in this situation and that I wouldn't be the last either.

You might be wondering how they helped me? Well, they got me to think about certain key things that then allowed me to get a better grip on my own needs and my own personality. If you are interested, they got me to think along these lines.

- What do I feel comfortable doing?
- What do I feel uncomfortable doing?
- How forceful am I in saying no?
- Why do I feel the way I do if I try to say no?
- What do I believe will happen if I do say no?
- How important are the various boundaries to me?

Just by coming up with my own answers to these kinds of questions, it meant that I had a better understanding of what my boundaries were going to be. It's amazing how many people have no idea on what their limitations are, so there's no chance of you being able to put them into place and then start your recovery from the abuse.

I would highly recommend spending time thinking about what you really want so you can then think about your boundaries before you then perhaps seek additional help to know how to implement them effectively.

Step 4: Putting the Boundaries in Place

Putting the actual boundaries in place wasn't easy for me. I understood I had tried to do this in the past and yet they just trampled all over them whenever they felt like it. I believed it was hopeless and a waste of time, but then I was clearly doing something wrong.

It's normal to look at the concept of boundaries and just feel that you are a lost cause with them. After all, if you continue to apparently fail at something, then you will clearly look at it in a negative way.

However, here's what I have to say to you. Don't give up on the boundaries concept. It's going to be a major thing that will really help you to change your life. Strong boundaries create space between you and the narcissist, so their abuse becomes more distant and, as a result, it loses its grip on you.

Look at it this way.

If you have a strong wall around you that you keep reinforced, then it's difficult for the individual on the other side of the wall to break it down or to still hurt you with things that they throw over. The wall is your boundary, and you need to make sure that the narcissist with whom you are dealing is on the other side of the wall.

But there was a problem for me.

The problem was that both narcissists understood that I had tried to introduce these boundaries at other times. One just completely ignored it and bulldozed right through my wall like it was made of cotton wool, which would normally make me feel useless and strengthen the idea that the narcissist was correct. The other appeared to accept the boundaries in the past.

However, I would then find out that this wasn't the reality of the situation, and they simply walked over them when the time suited them. To them, pretending that they respected my wishes was part of the game that was being played.

So, I had to get better at that game.

Getting Help to Change My Thinking

You must remember that narcissists are good at getting you to think and feel in the manner that they want you to. When this happens over an extended period, and my experience was years in the making, then what will then occur is you develop your own sense of incorrect thinking and thoughts.

The problem is that I was unaware that my thought processes were wrong, but that's common with abuse victims. You are drawn into this kind of game without even understanding it's a game and you are simply a pawn or toy to be played with.

This, for me, was hard. Patterns of thinking cannot be changed overnight. You have been fine-tuned to think and react in a certain way by the person perpetrating the abuse. Any attempts to do something different will have been hit by a bad reaction that shocked you back into their way of thinking.

This is wrong. Not only that, but I know from myself that it is damaging to the psyche and the soul. I should know, for my psyche and soul was damaged.

So, what did I do to cope with this?

Well, clearly my approach could be different to what you end up doing. Our situations are all unique. The way in which we deal with things will be unique to us. However, I can only tell what worked for me in the hope that you may look at it and feel that you should give it a shot as well.

After all, there's no harm in trying it because if it works, then great. If it doesn't then don't give up hope as it is just a case of you trying something slightly different.

The Advantages of Medication

First, I had to come to terms with the fact that the abuse had, in fact, made me depressed. It made me depressed just finding this out as I am now fully aware that I put off doing various things and changed aspects of my life to suit the narcissists I was dealing with.

I lost out on things due to putting the apparent 'needs' of others before my own, something that the narcissist would be unable to genuinely understand.

Now, some people are against the idea of taking medication for anything, but I know that it made a difference for me. It also helps in more ways than one and I'll explain how.

With me being depressed, it clouded my judgment as depression tends to do. Having impaired judgment when dealing with a narcissist won't exactly make anything easier. It will make it more difficult than ever before.

Depression brings on anxiety in me. The physical feelings, the apathy, all those negative things associated with it meant that I would continue to be a potential tool to be used by the narcissist.

Hardly a good situation to be in when you are trying to overcome the issues of abuse.

Medication did help with that. It removed so much of the brain fog that surrounded me. It allowed me to come to terms with my own thoughts and my own issues, so I could deal with them and make myself less attractive to the narcissist.

It helped, but even though it can take away various things, it cannot take away the incorrect thought processes that you have running through your head.

The Power of CBT

Now, for me in getting over the abuse side of things, I turned to CBT. This might work for you; it might not. However, I do recommend getting professional therapy whether it be this, hypnotherapy, or even just counseling and getting things off your chest.

CBT had a very specific point to it. The point was to change my thought patterns to something that was far more positive and helpful to me.

This wasn't a quick fix by any means. It did give me the chance to talk over aspects of the abuse and narcissism with a trained professional (the person doing the CBT was also a trained psychologist) who could give me an insight into what was really going on.

I found that this approach really did go back to basics, but there was a need to effectively reprogram me and to start to view myself in a better light. Remember, I had spent years trying to appease individuals that were pretty much impossible to appease. In other words, fighting a losing battle without truly understanding it.

In my case, CBT did work. It's still a work in progress, and I'll explain why shortly. However, I discovered that it did change my thought patterns and, at the same time, boosted my self-esteem which was sorely lacking. Of course, thinking more positively and understanding that you do have the right to say no and not feel bad about it is a good thing at various times.

Hardly attributes that would be attractive to a narcissist.

This is something that I would recommend to anybody that finds themselves in a situation whereby they are being abused by a narcissist. During the time spent trying to deal with them, so much of your own self is going to be stripped away bit by bit until you become a shadow of who you should really be.

Therapy of any kind helps you to rebuild that part of your personality. It answers so many questions that you will begin to have in your mind and believe me there will be a lot once you make that decision that you will no longer allow yourself to be subjected to this abusive relationship.

Recap on How Boundaries were Put in Place

OK, I admit that I have spoken extensively about the actions I had to take, and I know that there's a lot to wade through. However, let me try to break it down into something that's easier to follow:

- Understand the boundaries you are putting into place.

- Understand why you are putting them into place.

- Make it clear not only what the boundary is, but why.

- Seek professional help to counteract the negative thoughts in your mind.

- Get advice from someone that has dealt with narcissists before.

- Do not back down.

- Do not come across as weak.

- Be prepared for battles and tantrums.

- Don't be afraid to deal with your own issues in any way you can.

I'm not saying you are going to be perfect. However, boundaries do then provide you with that all-important breathing space to allow you to make real progress regarding your own self. The narcissist will always try to circumvent your boundaries, but as long as you learn how to be resolute, then there shouldn't be too much of an issue.

Step 5: Accepting it's a Toxic Relationship

No matter how close to you the narcissist is, there's a very real need for you to come to terms with the fact that the relationship as you know it is toxic. Anything that is abusive could be classed as this, but the issue is that you will often struggle to comprehend that someone close to you could ever be like this.

Well, they can because a narcissist doesn't think like the rest of us.

For me, that dawning in my mind that even though I was becoming ill due to all the pressure and demands, and yet they continued to do it, really highlighted that it was toxic.

If I'm honest, this was tough to accept. It's one of those things where you must deal with that disappointment you are feeling simply because someone isn't quite what you thought. However, someone once said to me something that was very profound, and it helped me to overcome that problem.

You might be feeling that way about the relationship and the way in which it has broken down, but the narcissist won't be doing that. They will feel sorry, but not the same way you do. They will be sorry for their loss, and the idea of you having a loss is not going to have even entered their mind.

Remember, they don't have true empathy especially when they want something. If they aren't hurting over this toxic relationship, then why should you? Why should you continue to go ahead and allow yourself to be abused in this way?

In my case, just dealing with this point and accepting it was another huge breakthrough in my recovery from the abuse I have received through my dealings with both narcissists.

It's Still a Work in Progress

I spoke about this being a work in progress and told you that I would explain it in more detail.

The problem is that I discovered the narcissists would keep coming back and trying out a new tactic as an attempt to pull me back into the old ways. Let me give you an example.

After severely restricting contact with one, which is always an option as a way of recovery, I then got an email out of the blue. The email itself was clearly an attempt to pull me back in. It opened with apparent empathy by asking how I was doing and hoping I was well. They also said sorry but didn't say what they were sorry for although I did see this as another attempt to pull me in.

There wasn't much else in the email apart from a question at the end that was rather personal, so I'd rather leave that out.

But here's the thing.

I had been quiet and waited several days before replying. I knew that they would follow up by making a request for help of some kind. In the past, I would have replied differently by asking what they wanted, etc, and that would have opened the door.

However, the work that I had done with the CBT meant that I replied in the correct manner. I avoided being drawn into a conversation, which would kickstart the entire thing again and made sure that it was clear they would be unable to get anything from me.

And guess what?

I got no reply.

To me, this was a success. I had made it clear that they wouldn't be able to pull me in, and they quickly lost interest in me and undoubtedly moved onto someone else. This was all part of my recovery, and it has shown me that I am indeed on the correct path.

Handling situations, as the narcissist will allow some time to go past and then try again if they aren't feeding off someone else, in the correct manner gives you the confidence that you are working through the abuse. You get stronger by the day and more confident in how you deal with things, and from that confidence, you become less attractive to the narcissist.

As I said, it's still a work in progress, but I am content with the steps forward that I have been able to achieve.

The Long Road

I've been dealing with my narcissists for several years now. However, that is just the length of time that I have been aware of the abuse aspect and how I was being used by them for their own greater good.

I need to stress that this is indeed a long road to travel along. It's not easy. At times it is dark, and you feel as if you are performing a U-turn and heading back the way simply because of how they will keep on trying to pull you back in whenever they feel like it.

But you need to be strong. Any survivor of abuse needs to be strong, and this is no different.

I've spoken about the way in which I had to effectively turn to my own self and heal from the inside before I could really expect to heal from the abuse. I sought help from professionals to help change my way of thinking, which had been damaged because of what they would say or do, and this helped immensely.

I'm not saying that it's going to take you years to get over this. It depends on so many of your own individual issues and not just the abuse from the narcissist. Also, the abusive nature of this relationship, which is toxic,

The Long-term View

My hope here is that I've been able to give you a sense that there is the very real possibility of recovering from the abuse that has been dished out in your direction from the narcissist in your life.

Just remember that you don't have to be in that position. You do have the right to look after your own self and put up blocks and turn your attention to your own inner self rather than what you are being told by others.

I must admit that it hasn't been an easy road to recovery. I'm still on my toes and accept that this is probably going to have to be the status quo for the foreseeable future. That might sound a bit depressing, but then I just view this form of depression as being an easier form to deal with than how I would feel if I allowed the abuse to continue.

It's important that you understand you are not alone in all of this. Yes, it can feel as if you are fighting against the world, but then that's what the narcissist wants you to think. They want you to feel hopeless and helpless as that then makes it easier for them to continue the abuse and control the situation.

Don't allow that to happen.

I would like to think that there have been various parts of my own story that resonate with you and the things that I did to counteract the abuse and to recover will maybe give you some hope for your own self. A lot has been covered, so I will now try to give a summary that will just make it that bit easier for you to recap on the main ideas.

- Accept that you are being abused. The way they act towards you is abusive and the sooner you accept this, then the faster the recovery can begin.

- Accept your own failings in this. Put simply, there will often be things within your own personality that have drawn the narcissist to you. Find them and get to work on resolving them to help aid your recovery.

- Get honest with yourself. Sticking your head in the sand serves no purpose other than prolonging your own agony.

- Be aware of when you have reached your breaking point. Once you do, it's time to act.

- Work on your own self-worth. There's a good chance that this has been stripped from you, so you need to rebuild your self-worth to then allow yourself to heal.

- Learn about boundaries. You may have tried this and failed. However, you were just doing it wrong or were not strong enough. Boundaries stop the abuse and provide you with the space that you need to heal.

- Get expert advice. I did on several occasions and in different ways. I sought help for my own issues including therapy to change my incorrect thinking. Narcissists are good at getting you to think along their lines over time, so changing it isn't easy.

- Remember it's a toxic relationship. It's not normal even though there will be times where it feels like it. You must come to terms that it's not healthy in its current state.

- Be prepared for the long road to recovery. Dealing with abuse is never easy and there's a good chance they have used some derogatory terms and threats towards you. Those scars cut deep and take time to heal, but they can and will heal if you are serious about doing so.

I do admit that I have to always be on my toes. My guard is always up, but it must be. Anything else and I worry I could slip back into the old ways. However, with the work that I have done on myself, and continue to do, this should become less of an option as time passes.

If you know that this is a long-term thing, then you won't feel so disappointed or fearful when the abuser tries to reel you in just one more time.

One last thing... In the spirit of raising awareness, I would like to ask you to leave an honest review about this book on Amazon. It really does make a big difference.

I also want to give you a chance to win a **$200.00 Amazon Gift Card** as a thank-you for reading this book.

All I ask is that you give me some feedback! You can also copy/paste your *Amazon* or *Goodreads review* and this will also count.

Your opinion is valuable to me. It will only take a minute of your time to let me know what you like and what you didn't like about this book. The hardest part is deciding how to spend the two hundred dollars! Just follow this link.

http://booksfor.review/narcissist

35226189R00061

Printed in Poland
by Amazon Fulfillment
Poland Sp. z o.o., Wrocław